THE HEALING POWER OF

CRYSTALS

CASS & JANIE JACKSON

Published in 2001 by Caxton Editions
20 Bloomsbury Street
London WC1B 3JH
a member of the Caxton Publishing Group

© 2001 Caxton Publishing Group

Designed and produced for Caxton Editions
by Open Door Limited
Rutland, United Kingdom

Editing: Mary Morton
Coordination and Typesetting: Jane Booth
Illustration: Andrew Shepherd, Art Angle
Digital Imagery © copyright 2001 Photodisc, Inc.

Title: CRYSTALS
ISBN: 1-84067-281-1

Acknowledgments: With Special thanks to Don Edwards, Tideswell
Dale Rock Shop for his invaluable help in providing the crystals for
the photography in this publication.
www.tideswel.demon.co.uk

IMPORTANT NOTICE
**This book is not intended to be a substitute for medical advice or
treatment. Any person with a condition requiring medical
attention should consult a qualified medical practitioner or
suitable therapist.**

THE HEALING POWER OF

CRYSTALS

CASS & JANIE JACKSON

CAXTON EDITIONS

CONTENTS

CONTENTS

Crystals are found all over the world, above and below the surface of the earth. Sometimes, smaller ones are washed out of caves by mountain streams, but most are to be found where they have been growing for millions of years, deep in the bowels of the earth. In these large natural caverns, the minerals condensed, gradually forming crystals. On a much smaller scale, crystals can be found inside hollow rocks (called 'druses') or even in stones (called 'geodes').

Left: amethyst crystals (far left), a geode containing quartz crystals (left) and a single large quartz crystal (below).

Below: the right conditions, and chemical combinations are needed to form crystals. They are said to contain not only the complete history of the earth, but also the wisdom of outer space and the entire universe.

HOW ARE CRYSTALS FORMED?

The right combinations of chemicals and conditions are needed. Quartz, for example, is made of silica and oxygen. Additionally, a temperature of more than 300 degrees C. is required, plus sufficient pressure – about 20,000 lbs per square inch – in the earth's crust. This combination of circumstances allows the liquid crystal to form. As it cools the liquid solidifies and the regular crystalline structure – an essential feature of crystals – is formed.

These stones can vary in size from microscopic but perfectly formed crystals to giants, such as the one three feet high and three feet wide, which is now in a French museum. Even more impressive is the massive single crystal discovered in India. It is six feet tall and measures three feet across.

EARTHKEEPERS

More giant crystals have been discovered in America, in caves 60 feet underground. These large crystals are called Earthkeepers. They are said to contain not only the complete history of the earth, but also the wisdom of outer space and the entire universe. Here we find the source of the belief that crystals are more than lifeless pieces of inert material. And from this conviction springs the whole world of crystal power, going back to the beginning of time and forward to today's latest technological advances.

Left: quartz (below) is one of the most versatile crystals used by man, being used in a host of electronic devices from quartz watches to computers.

'KRUSTALLOS'

WHAT DOES THE WORD 'CRYSTAL' MEAN?

The name 'crystal' is derived from the ancient Greek word *krustallos* meaning 'clear ice'. It seems likely that early allusions to crystals referred to clear quartz. The ancients also called it 'Holy Ice', believing that a crystal was frozen holy water spilled out from Heaven. Another belief was that a crystal had been made from water frozen at such a low temperature that it could never thaw out. Quartz was one of the first crystals to be used by man, and it is now one of the most important, being used as it is in a host of electronic devices, from quartz watches to computers.

Right: tumbled malachite, an amorphous crystal whose structure can only be seen under a microscope.

Below right: a single terminated quartz crystal and tumbled moss agate (below right).

WHAT IS A CRYSTAL?

Most people use the word 'crystal' to mean a stone with a crystalline shape – that is, like a small piece of glass, faceted and sparkling. Throughout this book, the term is used to refer to some of the minerals, commonly known as crystals, that can be used by man. Where appropriate the words gemstone, gem, jewel or stone may have also been used.

TYPES OF CRYSTALS

There are two main types of crystals, clear (such as clear quartz and ruby) and opaque (such as jade and lapis lazuli). Some crystals, such as opal and tiger's eye, do not appear to fall into either of these categories. This type of stone is often called opalescent.

The next classification of stone is either crystalline or amorphous. The crystalline type – such as amethysts or citrine – possesses a natural faceted shape when it is mined. Carnelian and malachite are examples of amorphous stones that exhibit their true crystal structure only under a microscope.

Crystals come in several different forms. A single terminated crystal is really a part broken from a large cluster. When a crystal comes to a natural point at both ends it is known as double terminated.

Sometimes, one crystal appears to be growing out of another, to produce what is known as twin crystals. These may be of equal size, but usually one is larger than the other. A group of smaller crystals growing out of the underlying rocky substance is called a cluster or bed of crystals.

Naturally faceted crystals are the most highly prized and consequently the most expensive.

Unfortunately, the current interest in crystals means that sometimes broken stones are cut and polished to create a shape that approximates to the original – just as precious jewels are faceted and polished.

Amorphous stones are usually broken into suitably sized pieces, then put through a process called 'tumbling'. This reproduces the same effect as the sea tumbling the pebbles against one another, and thus rounds and smooths them. When tumbling crystals the process is taken one stage further so that the stones become highly polished.

Crystals, then, can be as opaque as the darkest bloodstone or as clear as the brightest diamond. The highest quality crystals are used as gemstones for making expensive jewellery. These are graded according to four Cs – clarity, cut, colour and carat (the weight of the stone.) The higher the grading for each of these qualities, the more valuable the jewel.

Since time began, man is known to have used crystals in many ways – some practical, some aesthetic and some sacred. In this book, we shall cover historical facts where they are available, but the full truth about these magical stones and their powers remains unproven. We can offer only the myths and legends – stories that have been handed down by word of mouth for centuries, yet which still fascinate the people of today.

Left: a selection of tumbled crystals, highly polished and very tactile.

Crystal amulets, talismans and charms have often been found in prehistoric burial grounds. Apparently such items were considered essential for the well being of the dead. Many of these stones were pierced so that the good-luck piece could be threaded on a thong and worn round the neck.

Left and far left: crystal amulets, talismans and charms have often been found in prehistoric burial grounds.

CRYSTALS IN ATLANTIS

The legendary land of Atlantis features prominently in any history of crystals. Since there is no proof that Atlantis itself ever existed, these stories cannot be claimed as facts. It is strange, nevertheless, to compare with modern technology the assertions that crystals in Atlantis were used as a means of communication, to store energy and to provide light and heat.

Left: a faceted single quartz crystal.

Right: a popular
impression of Atlantis.
The Atlanteans kept
secret records on or in
quartz crystals (below).
The crystals were distin-
guished by small,
perfectly formed
triangular markings on
the surface, and were
called record keepers.

RECORD KEEPERS

One interesting suggestion is that the Atlanteans kept secret records on or in quartz crystals. This, they believed, ensured that such records would remain intact forever, with no risk of destruction through age or local catastrophe. These crystals were distinguished by small, perfectly formed triangular markings on the surface, and were called record keepers. It is possible to find quartz crystals bearing these triangular patterns and they are greatly prized.

AARON'S BREASTPLATE

In the Bible (*Exodus*, 39) we find strict instructions about the crystals to be used in the breastplate the Lord had instructed Moses to produce for Aaron, the priest. There were to be four rows of stones – in the first, a sardius, a topaz and a carbuncle, in the second an emerald, a sapphire and a diamond. The third row consisted of a jacinth, an agate and an amethyst, and the fourth row carried a beryl, an onyx and a jasper.

All these stones were set in gold filigree and each was engraved with a seal, one for each of the 12 tribes of Israel. It is obvious that each of the crystals named held a special meaning and purpose, perhaps aligned to the particular tribe it represented.

Exodus 39 presents a vivid picture of the magnificence of the garments provided for the priests and of the Tabernacle itself.

THE BOY PHARAOH

The opening of the magnificent tomb of Tutankhamun proved beyond all possible doubt the reverence with which the Ancient Egyptians regarded jewels. They believed that in addition to indicating the wealth and majesty of the pharaoh, the stones possessed mystical charms to protect him in the after-life.

Tutankhamun's sarcophagus was made from quartzite. Within the linen bandages that swathed his body were 143 jewelled amulets. Perhaps it is not surprising that tomb-robbers desecrated the graves of the pharaohs, knowing that the rulers were so sumptuously interred. Bearing in mind the supposed magical powers of all precious stones, we may even wonder about the notorious curse claimed to have had such devastating effects on those who disturbed the young pharaoh's last sleep.

LOOKING INTO THE FUTURE

In America, both the Mayans and the Indians used crystals as a means to diagnose illness as well as cure it. Indians of the Cherokee tribe also used crystals for divination. Believing the crystal to be a living entity, they first nourished it by rubbing it in deer's blood. Medicine men in the American Indian tribes claimed to be able to foresee the future by gazing into the depths of large faceted crystals, just as today's fortune-tellers gaze into crystal balls.

Above: in America the Indians used crystals for diagnosing illness and curing it, as well as for divination.

Left: Tutankhamun's sarcophagus was made from quartzite.

Below: today's fortune-tellers still gaze into crystal balls.

CRYSTALS AND THE CHAKRAS

Within the body of every human being are to be found seven centres of energy, known as the chakras. The word 'chakra' is a Sanskrit term meaning 'wheel of light'. Thus, the chakras are often illustrated as turning or vibrating wheels or – more romantically – as lotus flowers. If we are to enjoy complete mental and physical health, these wheels need to be perfectly balanced. When the life force or the flow of energy between the chakras is blocked or restricted, crystals can often be used to correct the problem. Simply expressed, this healing occurs when the vibrations emanating from the crystals are balanced with the vibrations of the chakras.

LOCATING THE CHAKRAS

These energy centres are not visible to the naked eye, but it is easy to locate them.

1 *The crown chakra*
– found on the top of the head.

2 *The brow chakra*
– found between the eyebrows.

3 *The throat chakra*
– found around the neck.

4 *The heart chakra*
– found in the centre of the chest area.

5 *The solar plexus chakra*
– found level with the navel.

6 *The sacral chakra*
– found at top of the pelvis.

7 *The root chakra*
– found level with the reproductive organs.

You may care to try a simple experiment to find the chakras within your own body. Simply place the palms of your hands an inch or so away from the general area of the chakra you wish to locate. (See list above.) Close your eyes. Breathe regularly. Try to visualise a soft white light gleaming between your palms and your body. Within a fairly short time, you will probably feel a stream of magnetism/power/energy emanating from the chakra with which you are working.

Some people achieve immediate success, but don't be disappointed if this experiment doesn't work for you the first time you try it. You may need to repeat the procedure several times before results become apparent. As with most things in life persistence pays – but it is important that you should remain completely relaxed. Tension and effort will result only in frustration.

Remember, too, that you are not playing games. You are dealing with your life force. Don't be tempted to show off your newly acquired talents as a party piece.

COLOURS AND CRYSTALS

All seven chakras swiftly respond to external forces of energy, including crystals.

Though all crystals possess healing powers, some are especially suitable for dealing with problems linked with particular chakras.

Each chakra is associated with specific colours, and, as will be seen, these are also the colours of the crystals most frequently used in healing. Most healers have their own preferences, based on their beliefs and philosophies, as to which crystal or colour should be used on each chakra. The following list is for guidance only and it is important to remember that the choice of crystals which can be used is extensive. Your own personal experimentation is needed to find the combination which works for you.

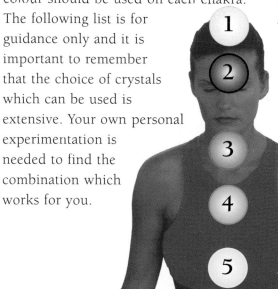

1. CROWN CHAKRA
Related colours – white/clear, violet or pure gold
Appropriate crystals – clear quartz, flourite, sugarlite

2. BROW CHAKRA
Related colour – purple or indigo
Appropriate crystals – amethyst, sodalite lapis lazuli, azurite

3. THROAT CHAKRA
Related colour – blue
Appropriate crystal – blue lace agate, sapphire, celestite, turquoise, aquamarine

4. THE HEART CHAKRA
Related colour – green or pink
Appropriate crystals – emerald, jade, aventurine, malachite and rose quartz

5. SOLAR PLEXUS CHAKRA
Related colour – yellow
Appropriate crystals – topaz, amber, tiger's eye, citrine or yellow zircon

6. SACRAL CHAKRA
Related colour – orange
Appropriate crystals – carnelian, sunstone or calcite

7. ROOT CHAKRA
Related colour – black or red
Appropriate crystals – obsidian, smoky quartz, red jasper, ruby, garnet, bloodstone or red agate

HEALING WITH THE CHAKRAS

It is possible and perfectly safe to combine crystals and the chakras for self-treatment.

The procedure is simple. Choose a time when you are unlikely to be disturbed. Ensure that you are pleasantly warm and that the lighting in the room is subdued. You may like to burn incense, light candles and/or have relaxing music playing in the background. The only essential is that you should feel happy with any ritual you care to follow.

The next step is to make yourself comfortable. Again, this is a matter of personal preference. You may lie on a bed, on the floor or recline in a favourite armchair. Breathe quietly and regularly for a few minutes, to still your mind. Then concentrate gently on the chakra representing the problem you wish to heal.

1. The crown chakra is associated with the pituitary gland, and hence with the entire glandular system which controls our general health. White or violet are the colours associated with the crown chakra, and the clear quartz crystal can be used to activate it; as can a violet crystal such as flourite or sugarlite. The procedure is simple. Hold a large pointed clear quartz crystal one or two inches above the head with the tip pointing straight down on to the crown. After a few moments, you may either feel a tingling sensation, or see coloured or flashing lights. This shows that the crystal is working.

The crystal should remain in position until these sensations begin to fade. Regular repetition of this procedure will ensure good results.

2. The brow chakra (the Third Eye) is associated with the pineal gland and its colours are purple or indigo. In many Eastern countries it is still customary to wear a jewel in the centre of the forehead. This almost certainly originates from wearing the stone as an amulet.

If you are prone to fears and phobias, then the application of an amethyst or sodalite crystal to the brow chakra is indicated. Follow the instructions given for the use of the quartz crystal, but hold your purple stone a couple of inches in front of the forehead with the point towards you. You will swiftly feel power flowing from the crystal to your head. This may be experienced as a short stabbing sensation. You may even feel the hairs round your eyebrows beginning to rise. Again, maintain the treatment until the effects begin to fade. Regular application of amethyst or sodalite in this way will help to dispel your fears and phobias.

3. The colour relating to the throat chakra is blue, and the use of a blue lace agate stone or a sapphire crystal is likely to produce swift results. This chakra is linked to the thyroid gland and therefore to the body's metabolism. It is affected by strain and stress – the most prevalent disease of the 21st century. To relieve this stress, hold the crystal opposite to the throat, pointing at the region of the Adam's apple. After a while you will feel warmth flowing from the crystal to your body, indicating that healing is taking place.

4. The so-called heart chakra is not positioned directly in front of the heart, but in the centre of the chest. It is linked to the thymus gland and its colour is green or pink. This area is associated with unconditional love, but also has links with any heart condition or the circulation of blood. It is said that use of a rose quartz crystal on the heart chakra will not only enable the user to express true and selfless love, but also it will increase resistance to infection in general. If it is employed correctly, you should feel a distinct tingling sensation. One somewhat disconcerting side effect may be a sudden flood of tears, because of the release of pent-up emotion. This is a natural reaction and nothing to worry about.

5. The solar plexus chakra is linked to the ego, that much maligned sense of self-esteem. A person with an outsize ego is unbearable, while someone who lacks self-worth can be equally irritating. Using a yellow crystal – either tiger's eye, topaz, amber or rutilated quartz – can provide the essential balance between these two conditions.

Holding one of these crystals a few inches from the solar plexus will generate a not unpleasant steady pulsing or throbbing sensation. As always, keep the crystal in place until this feeling subsides.

6. The sacral chakra is linked with the production of adrenalin — the powerful substance that gives you your 'get-up-and-go'. The adrenals, which produce adrenalin, are to be found on top of the kidneys, in what is known as the sacral region. The activation of this sixth chakra will enhance the user's energy, both physical and mental. Orange is the colour associated with the sacral chakra, and suitable crystals are carnelian or sunstone. Point the crystal towards the body at about

the level of the navel. You should feel a sensation of tingling and/or warmth. This will lead to a feeling of total physical and mental relaxation.

OTHER METHODS

Some practitioners prefer to place the appropriate crystals directly on to the body in the area of the chakra involved. This system is equally as effective as the one described above. This method will be found most powerful if the crystal is placed on the appropriate chakra while you lay down. It can be left there to do its work while you can relax more fully, not having to hold the crystal. To obtain the best effect, lay the crystal on your skin, rather than on top of your clothing. This type of healing is completely safe. The technique is simple, but the results can be extremely powerful.

7. The root chakra, found at the base of the abdomen, is linked to our sexual attitudes. frigidity, infertility and even, in some cases, mental stability. Its colours are black or red. The crystals that activate this chakra are obsidian, smoky quartz, red jasper, ruby, garnet, bloodstone or red agate.

Directing the crystal towards the root chakra should produce a sensation of heat at the point of focus in the body, together with a releasing of tension throughout the lower abdomen.

In researching other sources of information on the chakras, you may well find that some books reverse the numbering of these energy centres, starting with the base chakra as number one, and working up the body to the crown chakra as number seven. You may also find that the names of chakras differ from those given here. This should not create confusion as long as you remember that it is the position of the chakra that is important. The names and numbers used are purely a matter of taste.

CLEAR QUARTZ

Clear quartz is also known as rock crystal. The distinguishing feature of this stone is its six-sided crystalline form and its complete transparency. Some of these crystals are milky in appearance, but none is coloured.

This stone is extremely popular and much in demand for a variety of uses. In fact, it is often called 'the all singing, all dancing crystal'. It's also the easiest crystal to find. The golden sands of beaches throughout the world are composed of tiny quartz crystals, stained by iron in the sea. Quartz crystals can also be seen sparkling in granite.

Some people consider quartz to have magical qualities, a belief that has persisted for centuries. The Greeks thought that it was holy water, frozen by their gods. The Japanese believed that it was the congealed breath of sacred dragons.

In ancient times it was also thought to bestow the power of invisibility. A specially cut quartz crystal was placed in the seer's mouth. As a secret chant was intoned, the mystic was said to slowly disappear.

Quartz was also once said to prevent bleeding when it was used as a sort of ancient styptic pencil.

Australian aborigines believed that their shaman's intestines were made from quartz and that he was able to project these crystals into other people. It is unclear whether this was considered beneficial or harmful.

Many crystals listed separately, such as citrine, amethyst, rose quartz and tiger's eye, are in fact varieties of quartz. Each of these possesses its own singular qualities, which differ from those of clear quartz, and other gemstones.

One variety that is much sought after is rutilated quartz. This is a clear crystal containing inclusions of long, fine golden crystals that look like strands of hair – hence its more popular name of Venus hair stone or angel hair.

Another type of clear quartz is outstanding in its clarity. This is known as the Herkimer diamond, because of its exceptional transparency and sparkling appearance. 'Herkies', as they are called, are mined only in Herkimer County, USA. Unlike most crystals, they have been formed in water, not earth, thus ensuring the clarity of the stones. Having no roots in the earth, they are usually double terminated.

Far left: The golden sands of beaches throughout the world are composed of tiny quartz crystals, stained by iron in the sea.

Left: The Japanese believed that clear quartz was the congealed breath of sacred dragons.

Below: the Herkimer diamond, a type of clear quartz, with outstanding clarity.

A beautiful legend explains why the amethyst is purple. The Greek god Bacchus was miffed because he thought that humans were not paying him the attention he deserved. He therefore decided to wreak his revenge by setting his lions on to the next human who crossed his path.

The unfortunate recipient of the god's wrath happened to be the fair maiden Amethyst. Hearing the poor girl's screams, the goddess Diana took pity on her and transformed her into a pillar of rock crystal, to save her from the lions.

Right: amethyst crystals vary in colour from the pale mauve of the single crystal (below) to the deep violet of the druse (above).

AMETHYST

This highly sought-after form of quartz has a distinctive purple colour, ranging from pale mauve to deep violet. Large single amethysts are rare. Some of the most beautiful of these crystals are found in clusters, known as beds. Others form the interior of some magnificent druses where a crust of purple crystals lines a rock cavity. Sizes vary, but rock-shops sell druses measuring up to about 18 inches high.

On seeing what he had done, Bacchus was overcome with remorse. He emptied his wine goblet over the crystal pillar, thus staining it that beautiful purple colour that we know so well.

Amethysts have always been associated with Bacchus. Goblets encrusted with the stones were claimed to prevent drunkenness. In fact, the Greek work *amethustos* means, literally, 'not drunken'.

Those who could not afford such valuable goblets dropped a single stone into their wine. They also believed that the amethyst would change colour if it were placed against poisoned food.

At one time, it was said that the Holy Grail was carved from this superb purple quartz. And even today, a bishop's ring is still an amethyst mounted in gold.

The Romans were firm believers in the stone's magical properties. Roman matrons thought that if they wore amethyst jewellery their husbands would remain faithful to them. This led to the belief that it was the stone of piety and could protect the wearer from sin.

In the Middle Ages it was used as a charm against infectious diseases. Even today, it is worn as a protection against illness. Amethyst is the Elevator, said to lift the spirits and enhance inspiration and intuition.

Below: tumbled stones of amethyst.

ROSE QUARTZ

This beautiful pink crystal is fittingly known as the Love Stone. It is usually sold as tumbled stones – stunning, highly polished pink pebbles. Larger pieces of rose quartz are available, but these are usually the rough unpolished stone. Clusters are rare and single points exceptional.

At one time, rose quartz was thought to be so powerful that aggressive people could not survive in its presence. Certainly it appears to have natural soothing qualities that calm the spirit and banish fear.

Right: rose quartz, both the tumbled and the rough unpolished stone. Thought to be so powerful once that aggressive people could not survive in its presence. It appears to have soothing qualities that calm the spirit and banish fear.

Below: the red colour of Alexandrite in artificial light, which changes to green when placed in natural light.

ALEXANDRITE

This crystal, also known as the Love Child, is very rare and highly expensive. In daylight, it seems to be transparent green, but this changes to red in artificial light.

Alexandrite was first discovered in the Ural Mountains on the birthday of the then Tsar of Russia, and was named in his honour.

AGATE

Known as the Fire Stone, this crystal is found in many forms, both opaque and clear.

Today larger stones are sliced in order to reveal the coloured bands that agate displays. Not all of these colours are natural. Many slices are stained so as to produce a wide variety of colours – some natural, and some not.

Perhaps the most interesting of the agate family is the moss agate, a transparent crystal with what appears to be fronds of green moss inside it.

Agates were used by the Vikings in a peculiar form of divination for finding lost treasure. A double-headed axe was heated in a fire and then stuck in the ground, blade uppermost. An agate was then placed against the blade. If it stuck there, no treasure was to be found in that area.

But if it fell to the ground, the seeker must search in the direction that the agate rolled.

The stone is named after the River Gagates in Sicily where Roman soldiers found pebbles of agate in the riverbed. They kept these shiny pebbles as lucky charms. From then on it was believed that the agate could 'turn the swords of the foes upon themselves'.

At one time, farmers used these stones as an amulet to protect their crops. To ensure a plentiful harvest, they tied agates to the horns of the oxen when ploughing the fields. The moss agate, too, was valued for its ability to divine the presence of water, another necessity for good crops.

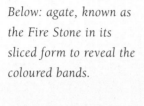

Below: agate, known as the Fire Stone in its sliced form to reveal the coloured bands.

Below right: tumbled stones of agate, the one on the right is moss agate; a transparent crystal with fronds of green running through it.

Left: a beautiful crystal of aquamarine; it name deriving from the Latin 'aqua marina' which refers to the colour of the sea (below).

AQUAMARINE

This lovely pale blue stone was beloved of the Romans who called it All Life. Through the ages, it has been known for its soothing properties. Perhaps this is why aquamarine earrings were so fashionable among the ladies of Ancient Rome. Apart from this, little is known about the historical applications of this stone.

Its name comes from the Latin *aqua marina*, referring to the crystal's resemblance to the colour of deep, clear sea water.

BLOODSTONE

This form of green jasper carries blood-red spots. Legend has it that it was formed when drops of blood from the crucified Christ dripped on to a dark stone. At one time, craftsmen carved the stone to represent the head of Christ, employing the natural red spots to indicate where the blood flowed from His head wounds.

This is yet another stone said to confer the cloak of invisibility. But wearing a bloodstone was not enough. It was necessary also to carry a sunflower. The connection between these two seemingly disparate elements is recognised only when it is realised that the Greek name for both the flower and the stone is heliotrope.

Below: bloodstone and a sunflower; the Greek name for both of these is heliotrope.

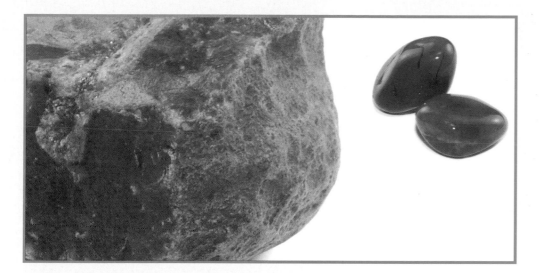

Left: carnelian showing its splendid colouring in the rough unpolished stone (left) and tumbled stones (right).

CARNELIAN

This crystal is known as the Friendly One. The name carnelian is said to come from the Kornel cherry, which it resembles with its splendid colouring. This may also account for the word sometimes being spelled Cornelian.

In Ancient Egypt, this crystal was called 'the blood of Isis' and was used for the protection of both the living and the dead. When a corpse was embalmed, a carved carnelian was placed in the throat. This was thought to protect the dead from any evil influences that they might encounter on their journey through the underworld.

Wealthy traders in the Middle East often wear a carnelian engraved with a prayer, as the stone is still thought to ward off envy.

By the mid-17th century carnelian was used against all forms of haemorrhage or fluxes, as they were called at the time. It was also used 'to defend the body against all poysons'. The method of treatment was to grind the crystal to a fine powder and then wash it down with a copious draft of whatever liquid was available.

It is claimed that if you place a carnelian in front of a bright light and gaze at it fixedly, you will be able to leave your earthly body and glide into the astral realms.

Below: in ancient Egypt a carved carnelian was placed in the throat. when a corpse was embalmed, to protect the dead from evil on their journey through the underworld.

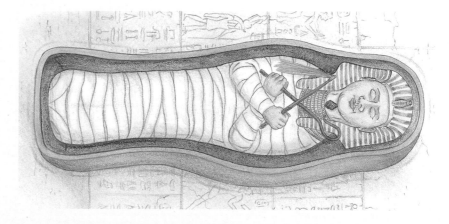

DIAMOND

The diamond is the hardest crystal known to man and is composed of pure carbon. On the Mohs scale of hardness, the diamond takes pride of place with a score of 10. No other crystal comes anywhere near it.

It takes its name from the medieval Latin word *diamant*, a variant of the Greek *adamas*, which means 'adamant'. And if you check the word 'adamant' in a dictionary you will find that it originally referred to a diamond or any hard substance.

Right: so hard is the diamond that it cannot be shaped in the same way as other crystals.

So hard is the diamond that it cannot be shaped in the same way as other crystals. For this reason, it is dealt with only by specialist diamond cutters. They examine the rough crystal carefully, to determine how to obtain from it the largest possible stone. Then they split off the unwanted parts of the crystal, as closely as possible to the final desired shape. Next, the rough diamond is bruted. This is a process of scuffing down the coarse shape, using other diamonds, rather as Stone Age man knocked flints together to shape them. Finally the stone is faceted by grinding it on a disc, using diamond dust.

The Romans knew of these techniques. Their cutters are said to have dipped diamonds in goat's blood, in order to make the stones more fragile and therefore easier to split.

Right: diamonds have become known as 'a girl's best friend', and is still the ultimate token of love.

In Elizabethan times, it became fashionable to mount a diamond in a ring with the point uppermost. These were called scribbling rings and were used to scratch messages into the glass of windows. It is said that Sir Walter Raleigh scribbled a message to Queen Elizabeth I in this way and that she replied in like manner.

The largest diamond found to date is the Cullinan, which weighed a massive 3,106 carats – approximately 20 ounces or 570 grams – when in its original rough state. If you compare this with the famous Koh-I-Noor diamond of only 108 carats you will realise what a monster the Cullinan was. When it was entrusted to the diamond cutters they said that it was almost certainly part of an even larger stone. It was finally cut into over 100 stones, the final total weight being 1,063 carats. Almost two-thirds of the original stone was lost in the process of splitting, bruting and polishing.

For all its beauty there is a dark side to the diamond. The ancients used it as a very effective means of murder, using the powdered gems as poison. Benvenuto Cellini, the famous Italian artist, sculptor and goldsmith, was targeted in this way. But the apothecary hired by the assassin substituted beryl – either aquamarine or emerald – which was not effective, and Cellini lived.

Conversely, the diamond was thought to have curative values. It was said to be effective against 'enemies, madness, wild beasts, chiding men, venom and the invasion of fantasies'.

Diamonds have become known as 'a girl's best friend'. And even today, despite its exaggerated market value, the diamond is still the ultimate token of love.

Below: the diamond is the hardest crystal known to man and is composed of pure carbon.

Right: in Roman times, the emerald was the jewel of the goddess Venus, and as such was used in rituals to arouse passion and love.

EMERALD

Emeralds have always been associated with the eyes. In dynastic Egypt the stone was used as the eye of Horus, in statues of the god. Subsequently the eyes of many images of gods and goddesses were made from emeralds.

Those who wished for an auspicious reincarnation made a point of wearing the crystal. Its green colour, reminiscent of Spring, was thought to bestow eternal youth.

The Peruvians worshipped a huge emerald – the size of an ostrich egg – that they called the Goddess Esmeralda. When the Conquistadors sacked Peru, Esmeralda was spirited away and has never been found.

In Roman times, the emerald was the jewel of the goddess Venus, and as such was used in rituals to arouse passion and love. This belief in its value as a love talisman led to the idea that the wearer of an emerald would be forever fertile.

The Emperor Nero is said to have had an eyeglass made of emerald. This was probably from Egypt, at that time the major source of emeralds. It seems likely, though, that the emperor's eye glass was made from aquamarine or a colourless beryl. The emerald is usually clouded by so many inclusions that it would be almost impossible to find a stone of sufficient clarity to use as an eyeglass.

At the time of the Crusades, green crystals became very popular, and were collected by the crusaders to bring back home. Most of these gems were, in fact, peridots – a chrysolite that is more common than the genuine emerald.

In later medieval times, emeralds were used to relieve the pangs of childbirth and were thought also to improve the memory. Apothecaries regarded the stone as something of a cure-all, alleviating all mental and physical agonies.

A two-fold meaning was attributed to the gift of an emerald. Although it was considered the emblem of true love, it was also used as a means of checking up on a lover's fidelity. Unfaithfulness resulted in the stone losing its colour.

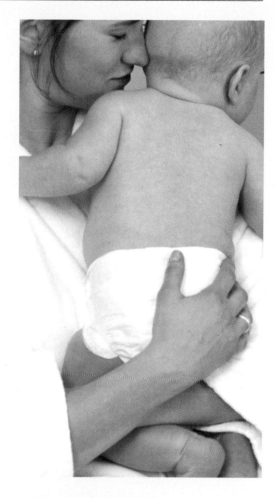

Left: in medieval times, emeralds were used to relieve the pangs of childbirth.

GARNET

The name of this crystal derives from the word *grenat*, meaning pomegranate, and was used, presumably, because of the resemblance of small garnets to pomegranate seeds. Larger crystals were cut and polished to produce the rounded stones so often set in rings. These, because of their bright red colour, were called carbuncles.

Legend has it that a large garnet carbuncle was hung in the middle of Noah's ark where it shone day and night, providing constant light.

In medieval times, a garnet was thought to defend the wearer against the plague. It would lose its shine in the presence of anyone who suffered from the illness. If the stone dulled over a period of time, this indicated that the wearer had contracted the deadly disease and would die.

The garnet symbolises hope and was regarded as a cure for melancholia. At the same time, if the stone succeeded in removing the depression, it was thought that the patient would then suffer from insomnia.

Garnets have also been used in warfare. As late as 1892 it was reported that the Hunzas in Kashmir were using garnets in their guns, believing that the wounds so inflicted would be fatal. This seems particularly strange in view of the long-held conviction that the garnet, like the ruby, could be used to staunch the flow of blood from any wound.

Right: larger garnet crystals were cut and polished to produce the rounded stones, called carbuncles.

JADE

Unromantically, the name of this beautiful stone derives from the Spanish word for colic. This dates from the time when the Conquistadors invaded South America. Many of them succumbed to colic, which the Mexicans cured by touching them with jade. Thus, jade was described as *piedra de ijada* which translates as 'stone of the flank' – the stone for colic. As late as the 17th century a piece of jade was worn on the hip in order to force out kidney stones.

Jade and jadeite are two separate minerals, both having a natural green colour. The most expensive is the apple green jadeite. This particular shade was so highly valued that one Chinese Empress decreed that all such jade, when carved, must be placed in the Imperial collection.

In China, jade was thought to protect the dead, hence death masks made from the stone. Jade ornaments became so popular that the supply soon dried up. This meant that jade had to be imported from Turkestan, more than a thousand miles away along the Silk Road.

Jade ensures a long and happy life for all who wear it and also enhances friendships.

Left: in China Jade (above left) was thought to protect the dead. It was used to make many ornaments and trinkets including lucky charms (above).

Right: lapis lazuli in its polished form and raw form showing the flakes of iron pyrite.

LAPIS LAZULI

At its best, this opaque stone is a glorious deep blue flecked with gold flakes of iron pyrites. The name comes from the Latin *lapis* for stone and *lazulum* from the Persian word meaning azure.

Lapis, as it is usually called, is thought to be the stone referred to as a sapphire in the Old Testament. There it is described as being 'sapphire sprinkled with gold dust', an apt description of lapis lazuli.

The ancients believed that blue stones, being similar in colour to the heavens, attracted insight and understanding. For this reason, Egyptian judges wore pieces of lapis carved into a likeness of the goddess Ma, who represented truth.

According to a prescription written in 1600 BC, lapis lazuli was one of the ingredients in a remedy for cataracts.

Right: according to a prescription written in 1600 BC, lapis lazuli was one of the ingredients in a remedy for cataracts.

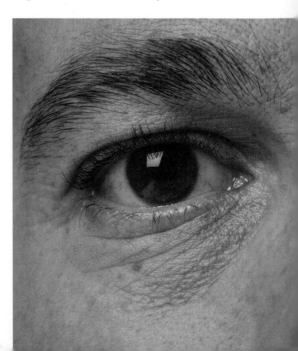

MALACHITE

This stone, with its bands of various shades of green, was named after the marshmallow plant, the leaves of which are similarly streaked.

In Ancient Egypt it was used for just about everything – as a medicine, a talisman or as a body ornament. Ground into a powder, Egyptian women used it as a cosmetic to enhance the colour of their eyes. Used in this way, too, it was said to improve the eyesight.

Left: ground to a powder, Egyptian women used malachite as a cosmetic to enhance the colour of their eyes.

The pharaohs' head-dresses were lined with malachite because they believed that the crystal would act as a channel for higher energies, thus making them wiser leaders. It was also thought to be effective in warding off evil spirits and to act as a protection against seduction.

Another name for malachite was the Sleep Stone. Anyone who gazed at it intently for a long period would fall into a deep sleep.

Left: malachite is named after the marshmallow plant which has similar markings on its leaves.

MOONSTONE

This variety of feldspar is found in Sri Lanka, where moonstones were thought to have been washed up by the sea. The best stones were carried ashore only once in every 21-year period – that is, three seven-year cycles of the moon. Hence the expression 'once in a blue moon'. The belief was that the stone's brightness differed according to the various phases of the moon.

The stone was thought to have three curative powers – one for epilepsy, the second for madness (or lunacy) and the third for lovesick women.

It was also believed that if a moonstone were placed in the mouth, then matters that needed consideration would come to mind.

The moonstone is still a sacred gem in India and is given by the groom to his bride at their wedding as a good luck token.

Right: moonstones were thought to have been washed ashore by the sea, and only the best ones were washed up once in a 21-year period. Hence the expression 'once in a blue moon'.

OPAL

The name opal comes from the Sanskrit word *upalas* which simply means 'precious stone'. It is also possible that it could derive from the Greek word *ops*, meaning eye.

The opal is not a true crystal, though its beauty surely merits the term. Its main characteristic is the fantastic play of rainbow colours inside the stone.

Opals are formed from liquid silica, taking on the shape of the cavity into which the silica flowed and cooled. This process has resulted in some unusual stones when bones – often from dinosaurs – became encased in sandstone and eventually decomposed. Liquid silica flowed into the sandstone cavity that was left, where it cooled and hardened into the perfect cast of a dinosaur bone, in opal.

There are many myths about these beautiful stones, one of which is that they bring bad luck. This may have originated from that connection with the Greek word for eye – perhaps it was deemed to be the evil eye. Despite this damning description, it was also known as the stone of hope and justice. Sorcerers were said to use opal to open the third eye and enter into the mystic realms.

Queen Elizabeth I refused to wear opals though she was reputed to own a great number. Queen Victoria also

Left: a cut and polished opal. There are many myths surrounding this beutiful stone, one of which is that they bring bad luck.

had a huge collection, made after the stones were discovered in Australia, but she seldom wore them. There is a story, though, that the Queen wore an opal ring on her way to the funeral of Prince Albert. During the journey, the opal fell out of its setting on to the floor of the carriage. Victoria is said to have cursed the opal roundly and ground it beneath her heel. Unlucky it certainly was – for the opal. Strangely, though, the Queen gave opals to each of her daughters as a wedding gift.

Opals always contain a relatively high percentage of water and, if allowed to dry out, they tend to crack. Keep yours away from central-heating radiators and other sources of heat to prevent this. If you visit a lapidarist you will find that he keeps his uncut opals under water.

RUBY

Most rubies come from Sri Lanka, but the best quality stones are mined in Burma. The rich red wine colour of these jewels is enhanced by electric light so it is always advisable to examine them in natural daylight before purchase.

In Ancient Greece it was thought that rubies and other crystals could be either male or female. Stones with stronger colours were said to be male while paler varieties of the same crystal indicated that they were female. The ruby is one of several stones said to foretell death. If its colour paled or changed to black, the wearer's life was in danger. Gem traders in Bangkok still believe that rubies are pale when first formed, then 'ripen' to their final colour.

Because of its colour, the ruby has always been associated with healing diseases of the blood. Eastern mythology calls it 'a drop of blood from Mother Earth's heart'. Rubies were inserted into small incisions beneath the skin in order to render fighting men immune from weapons made of steel. A ruby placed within a wound was believed to prevent a warrior from bleeding to death. It is claimed that Rasputin used a ruby to treat the haemophiliac son of Tsar Nicholas II of Russia.

One jewel that glitters in the British Imperial State crown is, in fact, considerably less valuable than it appears. The large gemstone known as the Black Prince's ruby is actually a natural red spinel. This famous stone was worn at various times by the Black Prince (Edward), Henry V, and Richard III. It is interesting to speculate about how a spinel came to be passed off as a ruby – and who cheated whom.

Right: a ruby in its natural form. Gem traders in Bangkok still believe that rubies are pale when first formed, then 'ripen' to their final colour.

Left: star rubies. These crystals have microscopic inclusions giving the appearance of a six-pointed star shining within the stone.

The famous Timor ruby, set in a necklace owned by H.M. The Queen, once belonged to Shah Jehan, the builder of the Taj Mahal. Owners before him were the great Moguls of India and the cold-blooded Tamerlane of Samarkand who stole the gemstone when he invaded India.

'Star rubies' are particularly valuable. These crystals have microscopic inclusions giving the appearance of a six-pointed star shining within the stone. The three crossed lines were believed to be the compassionate spirits of Faith, Hope and Destiny, who had been imprisoned in the jewel. Lucky was the man who possessed such a stone, for he would also possess those qualities.

Right: the most sought-after and hence most expensive colour of a saphire is cornflower blue.

SAPPHIRE

The sapphire's name originated from the Greek word *sappheiros*, which, oddly enough, also means lapis lazuli. One can only assume that the reference was to the colour of the stone. The most sought-after and hence most expensive colour is cornflower blue, though most stones sold today are much darker. Green, orange, yellow, pink and violet sapphires have been found. Most highly prized is the star sapphire, believed to bring good fortune to its owner.

Like several other stones, the sapphire was believed to change colour on certain occasions.

If the stone was seen to turn from blue to purple, the presence of a charlatan or impostor was indicated.

In Ancient Greece, it was compulsory to wear a sapphire when consulting the Oracle at the shrine of Apollo. It was thought that the stone would in some way help to explain the hidden meanings of the Oracle's prophecies. The blue sapphire was known to all Buddhists as 'the stone of stones', as it was said to create a desire for prayer. Hindus believed that it would bestow upon them the favours of their gods.

A talisman made for the wife of the Emperor Charlemagne consisted of two large sapphires, one round and one square, set back to back in a piece of the true cross. The purpose of this charm was to ensure Charlemagne's fidelity and it is said that his love for her never diminished.

Saint Edward's sapphire, another jewel now in the British Imperial State crown, was originally set in a ring worn by Edward the Confessor. Legend has it that on one occasion a beggar seeking alms accosted the king. Because Edward had no money on him, he gave the man his sapphire ring.

Many years later, some travellers brought back the ring. They said that its owner had died and that his last words were that he would, in a short time, see Edward in Paradise.

The king took this to be an omen of his own death, which became a self-fulfilling prophecy. His body was interred in Westminster Abbey, wearing the sapphire ring that had been handed to the beggar man so long ago.

Almost 200 years later his coffin was opened. It was found that his body was perfectly preserved. The ring was removed and, for many years, it remained in Westminster Abbey, where it was claimed that all who touched it would be healed. Only much later was the sapphire removed and placed in the crown.

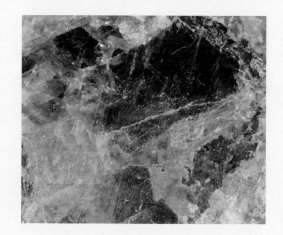

Above: sodalite was first found in Greenland at the end of the 18th century

SODALITE

Easily confused at first glance with lapis lazuli, this stone was first found in Greenland at the end of the 18th century. Though its deep violet colour is similar to that of lapis lazuli, the difference is immediately noticeable when the stones are put side by side. The two stones have completely different characteristics, and hence different uses, and it is important not to confuse them.

TIGER'S EYE

This beautiful tumbled crystal is a prime example of chatoyancy. This means that the stone bears a band of colour that appears to move beneath the surface. In tiger's eye, the base colour is brown with stripes of yellow and brilliant gold, much resembling the eye of a tiger.

This stone is one of two types of cat's eye crystals. Its lesser-known partner is hawk's eye, which has light blue bands glistening beneath the deep blue base colour.

In India, even today, the tiger's eye is used as a charm, which it is hoped, will ensure that the wearer overcomes any financial difficulties.

Of all the crystals, tiger's eye is the one mainly associated with children. It is said to cure many childish ailments and to protect children from evil influences.

A tiger's eye crystal is useful to have around when trying to get to grips with some awkward problem, as it will help you to pay attention to detail. It may also encourage you to see the lighter side of life, being the only crystal supposed to promote a sense of humour and minimise character flaws.

And finally, a tiger's eye placed near the entrance to your home is said to act as a household guardian.

Left: the beautiful tumbled stones of tigers eye and (below left) in its natural unpolished form.

TOPAZ

The name topaz comes to us by a roundabout route, via the Roman philosopher Pliny. At one time the only known source of the stone we now call topaz was an island in the Red Sea. For some reason this island was thought to float, and hence be difficult to find. When he heard of this, Pliny called the isle *topazein* which means 'to conjecture'. This island is now identified as the Isle of Zebigert, east of Aswan, in Egypt.

Nowadays, most topaz crystals come from Brazil and colours range from pale sherry to green. Lemon-coloured topaz is known as citrine, often called 'false topaz'. This is one crystal that should be kept in a jewellery box, as the colour does tend to fade on exposure to light. Tiny white topaz crystals are found on St. Michael's Mount, in Cornwall. The darker golden brown variety found in Scotland is called cairngorm. True pink topaz is very rare and nowadays is often created by heating the brown variety.

The one colour that is now recognised as true topaz is a clear golden crystal that has become known as imperial topaz.

Legend has it that in its natural habitat, topaz glows in the dark. It is said that miners marked the position of the stones at night and then collected them later, in daylight.

The topaz is an extremely useful and versatile stone. The Greeks mounted the crystals on divining rods and used them to locate gold, and the Romans considered topaz a protection against spells and black magic. They also believed that this crystal cured lunacy, frenzy and anger. Eastern mystics claimed that topaz helped them to make contact with the astral plane.

Right: topaz crystals vary in colour from pale sherry to green as well as a clear golden crystal that has become known as imperial topaz.

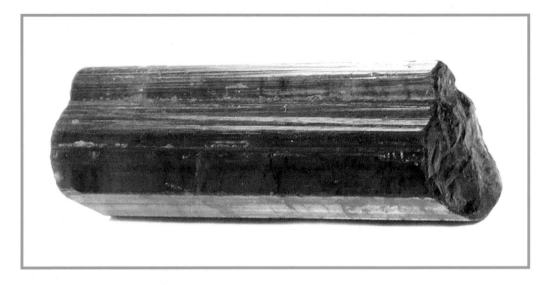

Right: The colours of tourmaline range from dark green (left) to pink (below).

TOURMALINE

The name tourmaline derives from the Singhalese word *toramalli*, which means 'yellow zircon', though, in fact, the tourmaline is not a zircon at all. Colours range from pink to dark green. Occasionally, crystals carry both colours – hence its other name of the Harlequin Stone. One form of the crystal, if cut, shows a pink centre with a green outer rim. This gives rise to the name of the watermelon tourmaline. It's not unusual to find tourmaline crystals showing chatoyancy – the cat's eye effect of bands of colour apparently below the surface.

Tourmaline exhibits an unusual electrical property. When it is rubbed or heated, it becomes positively charged at one end, and negatively charged at the other. This makes it into a unique crystal magnet.

At one time it was believed that tourmaline was transported to earth from higher realms – a gift from outer space. The object of this gift was to help mankind to attain a higher state of consciousness, in order to build a 'tourmaline bridge' between the different multidimensional worlds.

TURQUOISE

The name turquoise means Turkish Stone. In fact, this delightful, sky-blue stone originated in Persia, but was exported and marketed through Turkey.

Beloved of the Egyptians, it was linked with Hathor, the daughter and wife of the Sun God Ra. This led to it being called 'The Eye of Ra'. The Buddha is said to have depended on turquoise when dark forces assailed him. Almost every nation in the world has at some time used the turquoise as a talisman against evil.

Mayans revered turquoise so much that it was reserved as a gift to the gods and used only to decorate their images. The famous Aztec mask of the god Quetzalcoatl is completely inlaid with turquoise.

Many American Indians still earn their living by making and selling turquoise jewellery. At one time, no self-respecting Indian shaman would be seen without his turquoise necklace that became almost an emblem of office. North American Indians believed that the stone's blue colour reflected the severity of their winters and that anyone who wore a turquoise would take on the harsh and ruthless characteristics of the weather.

In the Middle East, turquoise beads are still woven into the manes and tails of oxen and camels to prevent them stumbling. Thus, the turquoise has become the talisman of horsemen, as a good luck charm for both horse and rider.

Ivan the Terrible of Russia firmly believed that a turquoise indicated quite clearly the health of the person wearing or carrying it. If the stone turned pale, it was reflecting the feelings of the owner, who must be sickening for something. Many thought that a turquoise would lose its colour if its owner should experience any misfortune.

ZIRCON

The zircon was thought by the Greeks to both lighten the heart and strengthen the mind of the wearer. Indeed, it ranked highest in their pantheon of crystals. The natural stones are to be found in colours ranging from white and red to brown and a beautiful golden colour.

This gem was used as one of the earliest barometers, said to turn dull if the weather was deteriorating and to brighten when the sun was about to shine. The wearer, it was claimed, became 'beloved of God and men', and would never be struck by lightning.

Zircons lose their colour when heated. It is then almost impossible for the layman to differentiate between the clear stone and a real diamond. Today, stones known as cubic zirconia are manufactured by the million for use as cheap, almost undetectable imitation diamonds.

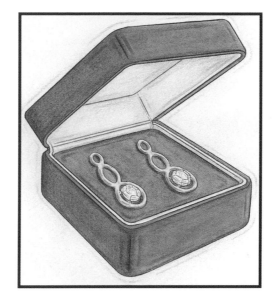

Left: today, stones known as cubic zirconia are manufactured by the million for use as cheap, almost undetectable imitation diamonds.

Left: he natural stones of zircon are to be found in colours ranging from white and red to brown and a beautiful golden colour.

Crystals have been used for healing purposes ever since man discovered them. At one time, a Doctrine of Signatures was formulated. This claimed that if a stone resembled in any way some area of the body, then it would be effective in curing disorders of that part. This was a somewhat simplistic view and obviously needed revision in the light of further research.

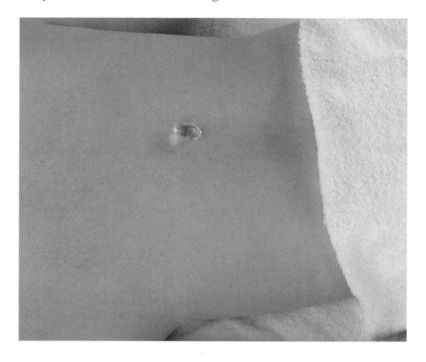

Left: crystals have been used for healing purposes ever since man discovered them.

It has long been known that our bodies need to keep in step with their own natural vibrations. Otherwise, we show signs of distress that can all too easily become dis-ease. Crystals, too, vibrate at different frequencies. Thus, if we can find a crystal that shares our own vibrations it will help to restore them to their correct frequencies.

Choosing the right crystal is important. Although the 'all dancing, all singing' clear quartz is considered to be the most powerful, you will usually get better results if you select a stone specific to your needs. Various crystals and the problems with which they are particularly associated are listed here. Check through this list before choosing your crystal.

NB: Although crystals are known to be effective for healing purposes, you should consult your doctor if any symptoms persist.

Right: When choosing your crystal take your time. You need to be absolutely sure that the crystal you select is not only appropriate for your purpose, but also that it feels right.

Far right: a selection of natural unpolished crystals.

BUYING YOUR CRYSTAL

Most towns have at least one New Age 'rock shop' stocking a wide variety of stones. This is an extremely personal purchase and one that needs a great deal of thought. We do not recommend that you buy a crystal by mail order.

When you enter the shop, you will probably be bewildered by the glittering selection available. Take your time. You need to be absolutely sure that the crystal you select is not only appropriate for your purpose, but also that it feels right. Ask the shopkeeper to let you hold it. Clasp it in your hand, close your eyes, and wait to see if you feel anything. Repeat this procedure using your other hand. You will know instinctively if this is the correct crystal for you. You may simply feel convinced that it's 'right'. Or you may feel a tingling sensation starting from your closed fist and possibly going all the way up your

arm. Sometimes, the crystal may even seem to move in your hand.

What if you feel nothing except a cold, inanimate piece of stone? Try again. Select another crystal and ask to hold it. Don't be shy about this. Take your time, and don't be rushed. The shopkeeper will appreciate that you know what you are about. Buy the crystal only if you are sure it is the one intended for you. If you can't find a stone that resonates to you, postpone the purchase until another day, or try elsewhere.

Let us suppose, though, that you've bought your crystal and now you are taking it home. Before you leave the shop, make sure that it is well wrapped and not rubbing against any other stone you may have chosen. This could result in an energy conflict between the two crystals that would be detrimental to both of them.

TAKING IT HOME

When you get your crystal home, remove the wrapping and examine the stone carefully. No two crystals are alike. Yours is unique. Note its facets and the way it refracts the light. You may even see rainbows of colour within it. Notice the variations in the size and shape of the facets. Look inside it to see if it has any inclusions. Hold it so that a bright light shines over your shoulder on to the stone and look for any chatoyancy, stars, or record keepers.

Don't try to use your crystal until you know it thoroughly and have prepared it as detailed below.

Above: single quartz crystals.

Right: examine your crystal closely, no two are alike. Hold it so that a bright light shines over your shoulder on to the stone and look for any chatoyancy, stars, or record keepers.

PREPARING YOUR CRYSTAL

Preparing comes in two stages, starting with the cleansing process. This involves more than removing any surface dust or grease that has built up on the surface of the stone. The cleansing rituals listed here prepare the crystal for your use and restore its energies. Several methods can be used. We recommend either of the following two. Use the one that suits you best.

Method 1

Place your crystal in a bowl, under a tap running cold water, and leave it there for at least 30 minutes, so that any negative energies are washed away. Then take it out and allow it to dry naturally, preferably in sunlight.

If you happen to have access to a stream, then place your crystal in the watercourse and leave it there for as long as possible. When you take it out you can gently wipe it dry with a soft cloth.

Method 2

The second method is to leave your crystal out in the garden in a heavy shower of rain – even better, during a thunderstorm. Be sure to place the stone where it is in direct contact with the earth. This will provide a grounding effect. As with the first method, allow the stone to dry naturally. If it can be left in the light of a full moon, so much the better.

Your crystal will need to be cleaned from time to time, but not too often. Frequent cleansing will dissipate its energies, rather than allowing them to build up. It will need cleansing if you have used it a lot, if it has been neglected for some time or if other people have handled it. Either of the two methods can be used. In time, you will know instinctively when cleansing is necessary.

Above: never place your crystal in a drawer or together with other crystals.

Left: when preparing your crystal, if it can be left out in a full moon so much the better.

Right: place your crystal on a clean surface where it can radiate its energy into the room.

TAKING CARE OF YOUR CRYSTAL

Never place it in a dish in contact with other stones. Their various energies will conflict and be weakened. Storing your crystal in a pouch or in a drawer will stifle it.

Far right: keep your crystal away from television sets or computers, both of which emit radiation that will interfere with the performance of your crystal.

Don't leave it in a box with jewellery or other trinkets. Place it on a clean surface where it can radiate its energy into the room, but ensure that it is not close to radiators or other heat sources. Keep it away from television sets or computers, both of which emit radiation that will interfere with the performance of your crystal.

Right: when programming your crystal choose a time when you know you will be undisturbed. Sit quietly holding your crystal in both hands.

PROGRAMMING YOUR CRYSTAL

You are now ready to programme your crystal. This process energises the stone to suit you and the use to which it is going to be put.

Choose a time when you know you will be undisturbed for a while. Sit quietly holding your crystal in both hands. Close your eyes and relax. Think about the crystal you are holding and what you want it to do. Imagine it fulfilling that purpose. Raise you hands, open them and breathe those thoughts over and into your crystal. Repeat the process until you feel that your crystal is fully energised and can absorb no more thought from you.

Your crystal is now programmed for your use. Take good care of it and, if you wish, talk to it occasionally. Send positive thoughts to your crystal and it will respond in an equally positive manner.

Be careful that your crystal is not mistreated in anyway. Don't encourage other people to handle it. Crystals always fascinate children, so keep yours away from inquisitive little hands. However, no permanent harm will result if others do hold your crystal. It simply means that you must cleanse and re-programme it before you can use it again.

The Cherokee Indians, who use crystals a great deal, consider them so important that they have a striking ceremony for bonding with each new stone that comes into their possession. First, they wash it in a running stream for about half an hour. After taking it out and carefully drying it, they give thanks for it by placing a few strands of tobacco or a few grains of seed – a token offering of wealth – on the crystal. Next, they purify the crystal by passing it through the smoke of burning cedar-wood. It is then kept closely wrapped in a cloth from the next new moon until the full moon. Every night during these two weeks the wrapped crystal is held close to the heart while the members of the tribe talk and sing to it. This could be likened to a mother bonding with her newborn child.

Although, by today's so-called civilised standards, this ritual may seem over the top, it serves to stress the importance of bonding with your crystal. Simplify this ceremony to suit your lifestyle, but do aim to form a strong rapport with your crystal in some way.

Left: the Cherokee Indians, who use crystals a great deal, consider them so important that they have a striking ceremony for bonding with each new stone that comes into their possession.

USING YOUR CRYSTAL

When you want to use your crystal – particularly for the first time – choose an occasion when you can be sure of being alone and quiet.

Background music is fine, but be sure that it is soothing and unobtrusive. Avoid music with lyrics – the words of the song will impinge on your thoughts. Similarly avoid the radio, when a news programme may suddenly replace music. Try to clear from your mind the clutter of everyday thoughts, especially if you have worries that are constantly harassing you.

Sit down and relax. Holding your crystal firmly in whichever hand feels best to you, rest that hand in your lap. Think now about what you are doing and why you are doing it. Be aware of any sensations that come from your crystal. Don't attempt to force thoughts or vibrations from it. Go with the flow and let it happen.

Now imagine a connection between the crystal and the difficulty for which you are seeking help. Visualise healing energy pouring out of your crystal and dissolving your problem. Retain that thought for a while. If it strengthens, hold it as long as possible. If, on the other hand, it fades, then your body has taken all the healing it can for now. Give thanks for the help you have received and put your crystal away for another day.

Right: when you are using your crystal hold it firmly in whichever hand feels best to you, rest that hand in your lap.

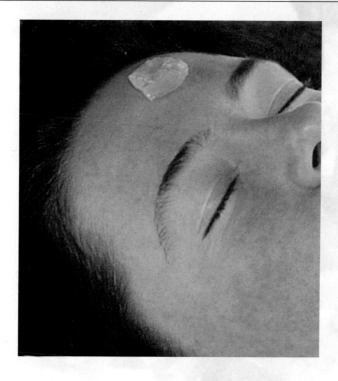

Left: it is sometimes beneficial to apply the crystal directly to the area needing help.

You may sometimes find it beneficial to apply the crystal to the particular area of your body needing help. To do this, simply place the stone next to your skin in that region and let it do its work. If your specific problem is associated with your head, lay back and place the crystal on your forehead. This works particularly well if you are using your rose-quartz crystal to alleviate migraine.

The methods we have mentioned will almost certainly produce good results, but you have no need to limit yourself to using your crystals in this way. Later in this book you will find other suggestions for using your healing stones. Don't be afraid to experiment. You will find that as long as your crystal is nearby, it will be of help. Try to keep it with you at all times – but if you carry it in a pocket or a handbag, wrap it in a clean tissue.

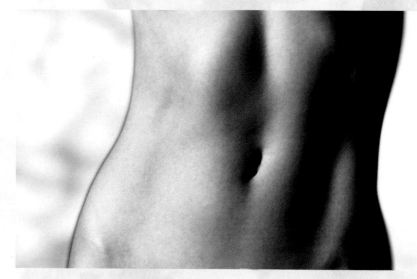

CLEAR QUARTZ

Clear quartz is the major healing stone. This is the crystal whose vibrations most readily resonate with those of the human body. It re-balances the body systems so that they work more harmoniously.

As you absorb its vibrations, you will feel physically energised and reinvigorated. You will find, too, that your thinking becomes much clearer and all traces of confusion are banished. Thus clear quartz affects the whole person, body, mind and spirit. For this reason, the quartz crystal is the best general healer. It overcomes fatigue and lethargy and restores you to the full joy of living.

Far left: clear quartz is the crystal whose vibrations most readily resonate with those of the human body.

Left: clear quartz affects the whole person, body, mind and spirit. For this reason, the quartz crystal is the best general healer.

ROSE QUARTZ

Rose quartz shares some of the powerful qualities of clear quartz, but it is gentler, more feminine and subtle. Clear quartz alleviates physical fatigue and mental exhaustion. Rose quartz removes the pain of the heart.

The colour pink has long being linked with emotional states and for this reason rose quartz is sometimes called the Love Stone. But it goes further than that. Rose quartz can lift the spirits in many ways. It lightens depression and swiftly dispels negative thoughts. Even feelings of utter despair succumb to its gentle persuasion. Placed on the forehead, it will ease a headache and is particularly good for migraine. Similarly, its soothing and calming effect will eliminate fear, anger, resentment, or jealousy. Rose quartz is the stone for dealing with emotional ills. Used in any fraught situation, it will bring peace of mind, serenity, and love.

Right: rose quartz can lift the spirits in many ways. It lightens depression and swiftly dispels negative thoughts.

Left and below: amethyst is a first-class remedy for insomnia, that scourge of troubled minds.

AMETHYST

This is the third of the great healing stones. Clear quartz affects our physical body. Rose quartz deals with emotions. Amethyst is equally effective in dealing with our spiritual wellbeing.

This crystal will bring you peace. It is a first-class remedy for insomnia, that scourge of troubled minds. Simply place the crystal under your pillow when you go to bed. You will drift into restful sleep. What's more, healing will continue as you sleep, easing the tensions that have caused your problem. Used in the same way, the amethyst will help if you suffer from panic attacks and it will bring relief in times of sorrow.

Amethyst can have a strong effect on your spiritual wellbeing. If you are seeking spiritual development and enlightenment, wear an amethyst on a chain round your neck or carry one in your pocket. You will soon begin to attain the higher consciousness that has hitherto evaded you.

Amethyst calms the spirit and helps you to deal with the traumas of life.

Right: hold alexandrite loosely in your hand and a wave of inner peace will wash over you.

ALEXANDRITE

Like the amethyst, this rare and beautiful crystal helps to restore the spirit after trauma of any kind. Hold it loosely in your hand and a wave of inner peace will wash over you, followed by a renewed awareness of the joy of living.

Although not as effective as rose quartz in dealing with the pain of headaches, alexandrite clears the head, aids the memory and improves eyesight.

Right: alexandrite (below) also clears the head and aids the memory.

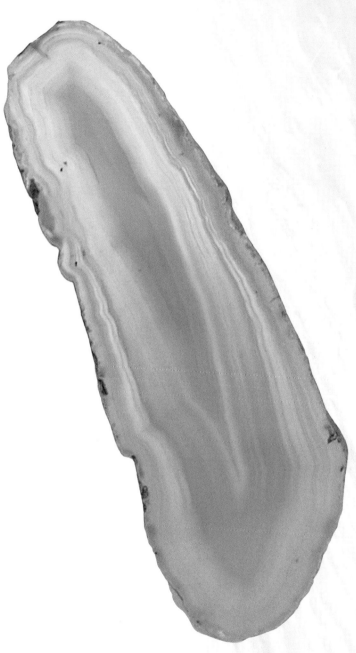

AGATE

Use agate when you need courage and confidence. It's widely used by drivers about to take their test, students sitting examinations, and prior to visits to the dentist. Athletes carry it for the feeling of determination it imparts.

This is the balancing stone par excellence. It will steady your nerves and protect you, increasing your feeling of security.

In the Middle East, tumbled agate stones are used as worry beads. The same effect can be achieved if you carry half a dozen in your pocket and finger them in times of stress.

Above: agate will steady your nerves and protect you, increasing your feeling of security.

Right: aquamarine (below right) is especially valuable if you suffer from any form of drug, tobacco or alcohol dependency.

AQUAMARINE

The lovely delicate blue of aquamarine is said to be the same colour as the Earth, as seen from space. This crystal is especially valuable if you suffer from any form of drug, tobacco or alcohol dependency. It calms your jangling nerves and strengthens your ability to make changes. Aquamarine is the tranquilliser crystal, bringing serenity and hope, no matter how fraught the situation. Used as a talisman against the dangers of the sea and seasickness, it may not calm the waters but it will steady your own reactions.

*Left: if you have poor
circulation and feel the
cold, bloodstone will
warm you up.*

BLOODSTONE

As should be obvious from the name
of the crystal, the bloodstone is
associated with all problems
connected with the blood. If you
have poor circulation and feel the
cold, this crystal will warm you up.

Heart disease, ailments of the spleen
and bone marrow problems all
respond to its influence, as does
anaemia. It purifies the blood and is
helpful in regulating the menstrual
flow during troublesome periods.

CARNELIAN

The carnelian has been described as the 'Friendly One'. If you're shy or inclined to be anti-social, it will help you become more gregarious. Although, in this sense, it can hardly be called a healing stone, it attained great popularity as an amulet. If you're introverted or lonely, you may well find that wearing a carnelian will bring you the blessings of happiness and companionship.

This crystal will also help you decide what you should hold on to and what you should let go of, a useful way to counteract indecision.

Above: wearing a carnelian (below right) will bring you the blessings of happiness and companionship.

CITRINE

This stone is similar in appearance to the topaz, but with different healing properties. Above all others, this is the crystal that will help to increase your self-esteem. It will also enable you to make quick decisions and to have confidence in your judgement.

Citrine links intuition with logic, an extremely useful combination. If you have lost your way in life, citrine will give you a new sense of direction, and the self-confidence to take a different, more positive, path.

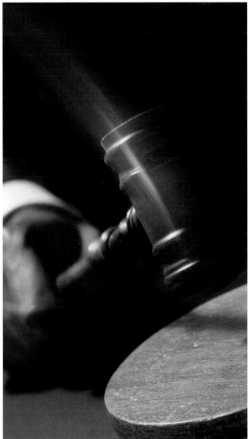

Left: the citrine (above:) will enable you to make quick decisions and to have confidence in your judgement.

DIAMOND

When it comes to healing, a diamond is everybody's best friend. It will solve your personality problems, boost your courage and ensure a long life. If you're unsure about anything, a diamond will dispense with uncertainty and leave your mind razor sharp. Wearing a sparkling diamond will overcome anxiety and strengthen your nerves.

For most of us, price precludes buying a large diamond for use as a healing tool. Fortunately, even a small stone, constantly worn, will be just as effective. You will find, too, that a diamond will enhance the properties of other crystals you may use for healing.

Right: wearing a diamond (above right) will solve your personality problems, boost your courage and ensure a long life.

EMERALD

Healers use emeralds in their work, to help them focus the healing powers, but anyone can use an emerald. It helps to improve the memory and, at the same time, reduces irritability and nervousness.

Wearing an emerald will strengthen your immune system and protect you against illness. Last, but by no means least, it will bring you rest when you're tired and weary – just the thing to use at the end of a busy day.

Above: wearing an emerald (left) will bring you rest when you're tired and weary – just the thing to use at the end of a busy day.

GARNET

This is an excellent crystal to employ when you are confused by emotional disharmony. A garnet will restore your self-control and allow you to see your problems in their correct context. It is particularly beneficial in calming hyperactive children, giving lasting results without harmful side effects.

A string of small garnets, used as a bracelet or a necklace, makes an excellent set of worry beads for alleviating many kinds of distress. Garnet will help you in two ways. It will ease your symptoms and will also strengthen your desire to be cured.

Right; garnets (above right) are particularly beneficial in calming hyperactive children, giving lasting results without harmful side effects.

Below: give jade (left) as a gift to the children in your family. Its delicate yet strong protective power makes it a wonderful first gemstone.

JADE

If you're feeling unsure about anything, jade will drive away your feelings of insecurity. Give it as a christening or birthday present to the children of your family. Its delicate yet strong protective power makes it a wonderful first gemstone for a child. It is also effective in the relief of asthma, which is today afflicting so many children.

Jade increases resistance to infection – a healing property that it shares with emeralds. Use it, too, if you suffer from kidney complaints or if you have digestive problems.

LAPIS LAZULI

This attractive stone has long been known to be effective in dealing with sudden mental affliction. Carry it with you if you are unfortunate enough to suffer from seizures or fits.

It is helpful, too, for small children who suffer from convulsions. Lapis lazuli is a mystic stone and is known to protect its wearer from psychic attack, so it's particularly important to use it if you have any worries in this direction.

Right: lapis lazuli (above right) has long been known to be effective in dealing with sudden mental affliction.

MALACHITE

Do you sometimes become so tense that you simply cannot relax? Malachite will solve the problem.

This stone balances the emotions and will swiftly nullify unwarranted fears. Just lay back, close your eyes, breathe regularly and hold this beautiful green stone in your hand.

In no time at all, relaxation will come naturally. You may even fall asleep. Because of its copper content, malachite is effective in relieving rheumatic pain and can also be used to reduce swelling or inflammation.

above: malachite (left) balances the emotions and will swiftly nullify unwarranted fears.

MOONSTONE

This crystal was at one time linked with the moon and thought to heal lunatics. Nowadays, it is seen as decidedly feminine and is sometimes called the Mother Earth stone. You will find it useful in a wide range of female problems, particularly those associated with the menstrual cycle.

It will relieve period pain, soothe swollen breasts and lessen fluid retention. Maintaining that same link with the moon and its cycle, it can help infertility and is even said to lessen the pangs of childbirth.

Right: moonstone (below) is seen as decidedly feminine and is sometimes called the Mother Earth stone.

Left: if you feel that you lack imagination and creativity, the opal can help you.

Below: uncut opals are often stored in water to prevent them from drying out and cracking.

OPAL

At one time, the opal was thought to be unlucky. It was even said to soften the brain. It was blamed for distracting people from logical thought and making them daydream.

Thankfully, this beautiful stone is no longer so maligned. If you feel that you lack imagination and creativity, the opal can help you. We now know that these qualities relate to the right side of the brain, and can be facilitated with the use of an opal.

Carry one with you; spend time admiring its beautiful colouring. You may be surprised at how quickly inspiration and original thoughts are released.

RUBY

As its colour suggests, the ruby is mainly used for healing blood disorders. If you have heart problems or just feel 'liverish' from time to time, you will find this crystal particularly helpful. It purifies and refines the blood. As a result you will notice a marked upswing in your energy levels, a priceless gift in today's busy world. If the pace of life has left you tired and insecure, this gemstone will also rebuild your confidence.

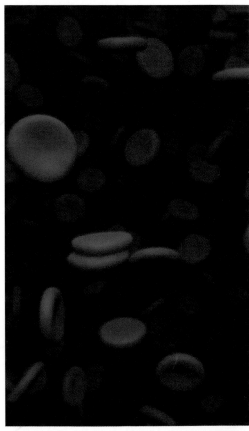

Right: the ruby (above right) is mainly used for healing blood disorders.

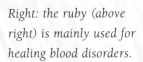

SAPPHIRE

The sapphire restores the balance between the physical and mental aspects of your nature. Because of its effect on the pituitary gland it is beneficial to the whole glandular system.

If you're inclined to be impulsive, this stone will help you to think before you act and thus will protect you from the painful consequences of hasty action.

The healing quality of crystals is not dependent on the user believing – or even knowing about it. If you have a friend who tends to be over-impetuous, the gift of a sapphire will possibly help that person to be more balanced.

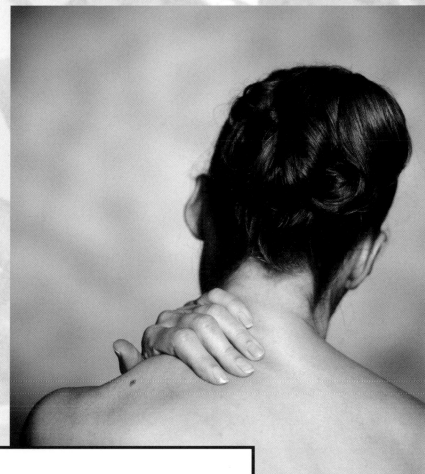

Above: because of its effect on the pituitary gland sapphire (left) is beneficial to the whole glandular system.

Right: If you suffer from high blood pressure, sodalite (below right) can help to lower it.

SODALITE

If you suffer from high blood pressure, sodalite can help to lower it. This stone is also effective in dealing with any type of fever. Sodalite is outstandingly helpful in dealing with depression. If you feel life isn't worth living, sodalite will swiftly change your views. It has been known to transform pessimists into optimists.

When you go to bed each night, place the stone somewhere above your head. The power of the sodalite will permeate your body while you sleep and often produces surprisingly swift results.

You will find that the longer the crystal is left in place, the greater will be its effect of calming the mind and dismissing negativity.

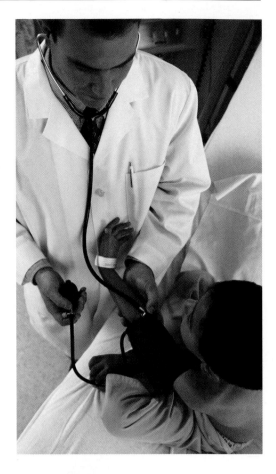

TIGER'S EYE

This beautiful golden stone radiates confidence and well-being. Simply gazing into the depths of a tiger's eye will convince you that nothing is impossible. It is particularly effective in dealing with psychosomatic disorders. Give this crystal to your hypochondriac friends to help them overcome their problems. Beautiful tumbled stones are inexpensive and readily available.

If you're under stress, this crystal will help you to develop insight and take a more rational view. It's good for digestive complaints, too.

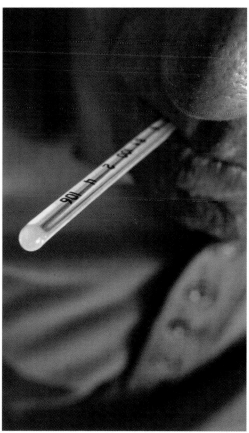

Left: give a tiger's eye crystal (above left) to your hypochondriac friends to help them overcome their problems.

TOPAZ

We hear a lot about the need for detoxification these days. Here is the crystal that will do it for you. Used regularly, it will remove from your body all the toxins collected from 21st-century living. As with most crystals, it achieves results on two levels – the physical and the mental. Not only will the topaz get rid of the poisons in your body, it will also relieve your mind of clutter brought about by the stresses of modern life.

Right: used regularly, topaz (above right) will remove from your body all the toxins collected from 21st-century living.

TOURMALINE

Astrologers say that the world is now entering the Aquarian age. Because the tourmaline is associated with the zodiac sign of Aquarius, this highly coloured crystal is known as the New Age Stone.

Tourmaline's unique gift to the 21st century is its ability to bring a sense of balance and tolerance, dispelling bigotry and misunderstanding. This crystal brings joy and happiness.

You will find that it has a strong protective influence in many areas of your life. If you're inclined to be nervous, tourmaline will enhance your self-confidence, enabling you to participate as fully as you wish in the opportunities provided by the New Age.

Above: because the tourmaline (left) is associated with the zodiac sign of Aquarius, this highly coloured crystal is known as the New Age Stone.

TURQUOISE

This beautiful blue stone is particularly useful if you are one of the many victims of eating disorders such as bulimia or anorexia nervosa. It can help you to eat sensibly and, at the same time, ensure that your body properly absorbs nutrients. On a more mundane level, it is very helpful with simple digestive disturbances.

The turquoise will protect you from environmental pollution. Compare this with topaz, which removes the toxins already acquired.

For some reason, this crystal's healing powers are much stronger if it is a gift from somebody else. So if you want one for self-healing, you know what to ask for when it comes round to your birthday or Christmas.

Right: Turquiose (below right) is particularly useful if you are one of the many victims of eating disorders such as bulimia or anorexia nervosa.

Below: zircon (left) is one of the few stones capable of helping those who have suffered some form of brain damage.

ZIRCON

This transparent gemstone is a powerful healer, giving off potent energies. It is one of the few stones capable of helping those who have suffered some form of brain damage. This includes any seizure, fit, spasm or paralytic attack.

On a less traumatic level, use of the zircon will ensure that you develop a more balanced personality.

Use it with care. If you're inclined to be delicate, it may be best to work with another crystal until your strength is restored. Be wary, too, if you use the stone to help elderly friends or relatives. Reduce the length of the healing sessions to no more than five minutes each day.

NB: Cubic zirconia may look like a natural zircon, but has no healing power.

CRYSTALS AND THE STARS

Ever since the first astrologers gazed at the night sky, certain crystals have been associated with the different signs of the zodiac. Generally speaking, it is beneficial to wear the crystal to which your star sign is related – commonly known as the birthstone.

Even better results can be achieved by selecting your own crystal from those listed below. All the signs of the zodiac have more than one birthstone. The following list contains three of the most commonly known crystals linked to each sign. Try each one in turn to find out which is the most effective for you. When you discover which crystal works best for you, clean it as previously described. Then keep it with you always.

What if none of the stones suggested for your star sign appeals to you? Simply choose a crystal that feels right for you and treat it in the same way that you would treat your birthstone. It's safe to assume that you are being guided to the crystal most likely to be of benefit to you at the present time.

Aries Mar 21 – Apr 20
diamond, ruby, bloodstone

Taurus Apr 21 – May 21
emerald, sapphire, lapis lazuli

Gemini May 22 – Jun 21
citrine, yellow agate, serpentine

Cancer Jun 22 – Jul 23
pearl, moss agate, clear quartz

Leo Jul 24 – Aug 23
tiger's eye, amber, malachite

Virgo Aug 24 – Sep 23
blue lace agate, sardonyx, rhodocrosite

Libra Sep 24 – Oct 23
azurite, chrysolite, jade

Scorpio Oct 24 – Nov 22
sodalite, opal, red jasper

Sagittarius Nov 23 – Dec 21
topaz, carnelian, aventurine

Capricorn Dec 22 – Jan 20
garnet, turquoise, smoky quartz

Aquarius Jan 21 – Feb 19
aquamarine, tourmaline, peridot

Pisces Feb 20 – Mar 20
moonstone, rose quartz, amethyst

Valuable though their healing properties are, there are many other ways to utilise the magic of crystals. For example, they can be used to bring tranquillity to your home, if you've been experiencing a number of traumas.

To do this, take several small tumble-polished rose-quartz crystals. Cleanse and programme them all together. Then go through your home, placing one small crystal in each corner of every room. It's particularly good to site them in the corners of windowsills. Your entire home will be bathed in the loving ambience and healing power of rose quartz.

If crystal power is needed in only one room, follow the same procedure, but use only four stones – one for each corner of the room. Tiger's eye, placed in the corners of your sitting room, will boost your self-confidence. Use smoky quartz in your office if you need inspiration. The secret lies in matching the power of the stone to the result you need – garnets will lift depression, jade will produce a happy atmosphere, lapis lazuli will create understanding when there have been opinion clashes, and so on.

Crystals can also be used to safeguard you and your passengers on the road. In most cars, the driver's

sun visor carries a small pocket – presumably for storing documents. Instead, use it to hold three small stones – clear quartz, rose quartz and amethyst. The crystals will be just above and in front of your head, while you are driving. They will ensure that you remain alert and clear-headed, and less accident-prone.

If you feel that your get-up-and-go has got up and gone, try drinking energised water. Simply place a clear quartz crystal in a glass of water overnight. In the morning, drink the water as soon as you wake. The energising power of the crystal will suffuse your whole body. Select the crystal according to the benefits you need. Rose-quartz essence, produced in this way and used as a lotion, will ensure a clear complexion.

Take your crystals with you wherever you go. As you establish communication with them, you will come to realise their extraordinary powers. Experiment with them. You will be amazed and delighted by what they can achieve.

INDEX